EDGE BOOKS

DIRT BIKES

Ricky Carmichael
Motocross
Champion

by Michael Martin

Consultant:

Dirck J. Edge
Editor
MotorcycleDaily.com

Capstone press

Mankato, Minnesota

Edge Books are published by Capstone Press
151 Good Counsel Drive, P.O. Box 669, Mankato, Minnesota 56002
www.capstonepress.com

Library of Congress Cataloging-in-Publication Data
Martin, Michael, 1948–
    Ricky Carmichael: motocross champion / by Michael Martin.
    p. cm.—(Edge books. Dirt bikes)
    Includes bibliographical references (p. 31) and index.
    ISBN-13: 978-0-7368-2438-5 (hardcover)
    ISBN-10: 0-7368-2438-3 (hardcover)
    1. Carmichael, Ricky, 1979– 2. Motorcyclists—United States—Biography.
3. Motocross. I. Title. II. Series.
GV1060.2.C37M37 2004
796.7'5'092—dc21   2003014752

Summary: Traces the life and career of motocross racer Ricky Carmichael.

Editorial Credits
Angela Kaelberer, editor; Molly Nei, series designer; Jason Knudson; book designer,
    Jo Miller, photo researcher

Photo Credits
Anthony Scavo, cover, 6, 8, 28
Kinney Jones Photography, 5, 13, 15, 17, 18, 21, 25
SportsChrome-USA/Justin Silvey, 11, 23, 24, 26

1 2 3 4 5 6 09 08 07 06 05 04

Table of Contents

CHAPTER 1

Motocross Champion

On September 1, 2002, Ricky Carmichael revved his Honda CR250R. He was at the starting line of the Steel City Raceway in Delmont, Pennsylvania. Ricky was racing in the last event of the American Motorcyclist Association (AMA) Chevy Trucks 250 U.S. Motocross Championship Series.

Ricky had won all 22 motos, or races, during the season. If he won both motos at Steel City, he would be the first rider to have a perfect season in AMA motocross history.

Learn about:
- A perfect season
- Championships
- Training

At Delmont, Ricky hoped to win both motos.

Winning the Motos

The riders in the first moto pulled away from the starting line. Ricky quickly moved into the lead. He crossed the finish line 21 seconds before the second-place rider, Tim Ferry. During the second moto, Ricky again took the lead. Ferry was right behind him. In the last lap, Ferry started to gain on Ricky. But Ricky sped across the finish line just 3 seconds before Ferry.

Ricky celebrated after crossing the finish line. He had done what no other motocross rider had done before. He had raced a perfect season.

Ricky is known for his speed during turns.

About Ricky Carmichael

Ricky Carmichael has been racing dirt bikes since he was 5 years old. He turned professional in 1996. Ricky races in both motocross and supercross events. Motocross events are held outdoors. Supercross races take place in stadiums and other large arenas.

Ricky is one of the shortest and smallest pro racers. He is 5 feet, 6 inches (168 centimeters) tall and weighs 160 pounds (73 kilograms). Ricky has not let his small size keep him from winning. He has won more races than any other rider in AMA motocross history.

Ricky is known for his speed on the track. Racing experts have different ideas about why he is so fast. Some say he lays down his bike very low as he goes through turns. Others say his small size and upper body strength help him guide the bike at high speeds.

Most people agree Ricky's hard work has much to do with his success. He has spent hours in training nearly every day since he got on his first minibike.

Career Statistics

Year	Class	Wins	Points	Finish
1996	AMA Motocross 125cc	0	13	32nd
1997	AMA Motocross 125cc	8	563	1st
1998	AMA Motocross 125cc	8	525	1st
1999	AMA Motocross 125cc	9	549	1st
2000	AMA Motocross 250cc	9	535	1st
2000	AMA Supercross 250cc	1	263	5th
2001	AMA Motocross 250cc	7	490	1st
2001	AMA Supercross 250cc	14	392	1st
2002	AMA Motocross 250cc	12	600	1st
2002	AMA Supercross 250cc	11	356	1st
2003	AMA Motocross 250cc	9	529	1st
2003	AMA Supercross 250cc	7	367	1st

CHAPTER 2

The Early Years

Ricky Carmichael was born November 27, 1979, in Tallahassee, Florida. His parents are Rick and Jeannie Carmichael. Ricky is their only child. He grew up in Havana, Florida.

Ricky's parents gave him a 50cc Yamaha minibike for Valentine's Day when he was 5 years old. He entered his first motocross race soon after. Ricky still remembers the first race he won. It was in Dade City, Florida, and he was 6 years old.

Learn about:
- First races
- Amateur career
- Heroes

Ricky has raced dirt bikes most of his life.

A Racing Family

Ricky's parents supported his interest in racing. Rick helped out as Ricky's bike mechanic. Jeannie drove Ricky to practice every day after school.

Ricky's hard work began to pay off with wins. When Ricky was 13, some people said he was the fastest minibike rider in the world. He became known for his desire to win.

A Dream Takes Shape

Ricky competed as an amateur for 11 years. During that time, he won 67 amateur motocross titles. These wins included a record nine AMA National Amateur titles.

Jeff Ward and Johnny O'Mara were two of Ricky's favorite pro riders. Ricky watched them race whenever he could. He also studied the way they acted when they were not racing. Both riders were known for their good sportsmanship. Ricky tried to behave that way himself.

Ricky was preparing himself to become a professional. The chance to get paid for doing what he loved came sooner than he expected.

Ricky hoped to have a career in pro motocross.

CHAPTER 3

Rising Star

In 1996, Ricky got the chance to move from minibikes to the bigger 125cc motorcycles. He entered the last race of the AMA 125cc Motocross Series and finished eighth. The AMA named 16-year-old Ricky its Motocross Rookie of the Year.

Ricky began racing full-time for Kawasaki after the 1996 season. On February 22, 1997, Ricky won his first pro race at the AMA East Region 125cc supercross race in Atlanta, Georgia. A week later, he won an Outdoor National motocross race in Gainesville, Florida.

Learn about:
- Turning pro
- Early wins
- Challenges

In 1997, Ricky started racing for Kawasaki.

"The fans just love that go-for-broke attitude the kid has. Carmichael will quit crashing before he quits winning. Until he gets to that point, he just needs to stay healthy . . ."

—David Bailey, ESPN commentator and former rider

Some people said he won there only because he grew up nearby and knew the track. They could not say that about Ricky's next win.

On May 4, Ricky easily won the Hangtown Motocross Classic in Sacramento, California. Ricky went on to win eight rounds of the 125cc Motocross Series and the 1997 national title.

Fan Favorite

Ricky gained many new fans after he turned pro. Some fans liked Ricky because of his small size. Others liked Ricky's speed and focus on winning.

Ricky did not always have the skill to go with his speed. He sometimes crashed his bike. In 1997, Ricky won more races than any other rider in the East Region of the AMA 125cc Supercross Series. But he crashed so often that he finished third in total points in the region.

In spite of his crashes, Ricky did well as a professional. He won his second AMA 125cc Outdoor National Motocross Championship in 1998. By the end of 1998, Ricky was ready for the challenge of racing 250cc motorcycles.

Kawasaki team manager Mitch Payton congratulated Ricky on his 1998 title.

In 1999, Ricky began competing in 250cc supercross races.

Something to Prove

In 1999, Ricky began racing in the AMA 250cc Supercross Series. Early in the season, Ricky was hurt during a crash. Because of the injury, he missed several races. When he returned, his highest finish was fourth place.

When the 1999 indoor season ended, Ricky went back to racing a 125cc Kawasaki. He won his third straight 125cc Outdoor National Motocross Championship.

In 2000, Ricky raced in the 250cc class in both supercross and motocross. He won nine races and finished first in the Motocross Series. But fifth place was the best he could do in the Supercross Series.

Ricky had something to prove when the 2001 supercross season began. He had won many motocross championships, but he had never won a 250cc supercross championship.

Fans wondered if Ricky was strong enough to handle a heavy 250cc bike on the tight curves of the supercross tracks. Ricky was determined to prove that he could.

CHAPTER 4

Beating the Best

Ricky trained hard for the 2001 supercross season. He hired a physical trainer to help him gain upper body strength. He also lost 20 pounds (9 kilograms).

The first race of the Supercross Series was in Anaheim, California. Ricky finished third. He won the next race in San Diego, California, and then finished second to Jeremy McGrath in Anaheim. Losing to McGrath was no disgrace. Many people consider McGrath the best supercross racer ever.

Learn about:
- Training to win
- Setting records
- The future

Ricky's strength improved before the 2001 supercross season.

Record Season

Something amazing happened after the second Anaheim race. There were 13 races left in the season. Ricky finished first in every race.

Ricky's 13 wins in a row tied the record held by McGrath. Ricky's 14 wins during the season also tied a record. He finished with 392 points out of a possible 400. Ricky's total was 64 points ahead of McGrath. Ricky was still one of the smallest supercross racers, but he proved he had the skills of a champion.

Breaking Records

Ricky kept winning in 2001. First, he won the 250cc Motocross Series title again. He then raced one last event at the 125cc level. His win at Steel City set an all-time record of 26 wins in the 125cc class. Ricky also broke the record for most wins in a season. He won 14 supercross events and eight motocross races.

Honda Motorcycles asked Ricky to join its racing team at the end of the season. Ricky agreed. He began the 2002 season riding a Honda CR250R.

"My family is behind me 110 percent. My mom is really tough, but it is the kind of support that helps keep me focused and driven toward my goal, which is to win races and championships."

—Ricky Carmichael, www.hondaredriders.com

In 2001, Ricky set a record for the number of wins in a season.

In 2002, Ricky won every motocross event he raced in.

More Championships

Ricky's 2002 season was even better than his 2001 season. After a slow start in the Supercross Series, he came back to win 11 of 16 races. That total was good enough for another championship.

In the Motocross Series, Ricky was undefeated for the entire season. He won more races that season than any other racer in AMA Motocross history.

In 2003, Ricky won seven of the first eight races in the Supercross Series. But in the last six races, he finished second to Chad Reed. Ricky won the AMA National Supercross title by just seven points.

Ricky continued to win during the 2003 motocross season. He won nine events and became the first racer to win four AMA 250cc National Motocross titles.

In 2003, Ricky won his fourth AMA 250cc Motocross title.

Ricky hopes to set many more racing records.

"These last four years have flown by. I've been so busy concentrating on racing that it's hard to grasp some of the things I've been able to accomplish."

—Ricky Carmichael, USMotocross.com

Life of a Champion

Ricky married in October 2002. He and his wife, Ursula, live near Tallahassee, Florida. Ricky also has a large home in Georgia where he built his own motocross course. He often practices there when he is not traveling.

Ricky still works hard at improving his skills, even in the off-season. Each day, Ricky lifts weights and runs. He then rides a bicycle to strengthen his legs. He spends the rest of the day practicing on the track.

Ricky works so hard because he likes the challenge of staying on top. He hopes to set more racing records in the future.

Career Highlights

1985 — Ricky wins his first minibike race.

1996 — Ricky competes in his first professional race and is named AMA Motocross Rookie of the Year.

1997 — Ricky wins the 125cc Outdoor National Motocross Championship in his first pro season.

1998 — Ricky wins the 125cc Outdoor National Motocross Championship and the East Region 125cc Supercross Championship.

1999 — Ricky wins his third straight Outdoor National Motocross Championship in the 125cc class.

2000 — Ricky wins his first motocross championship in the 250cc class.

2001 — Ricky wins both the AMA National Supercross Championship and the 250cc Motocross Championship.

2002 — Ricky wins every moto in all 12 races of the AMA Motocross Series; he also wins 11 of 16 races to win the AMA Supercross Series.

2003 — Ricky wins his third AMA Supercross Championship and his fourth AMA 250cc Motocross Championship.

Glossary

amateur (AM-uh-chur)—an athlete who does not earn a living from competing in a sport

mechanic (muh-KAN-ik)—a person who is skilled at repairing vehicles or machinery

moto (MOH-toh)—a single motocross race; each event includes two motos.

professional (pruh-FESH-uh-nuhl)—an athlete who earns a living from competing in a sport

rookie (RUK-ee)—a first-year athlete

series (SIHR-eez)—a group of races; racers earn points based on how they finish in each race.

sportsmanship (SPORTS-muhn-ship)—fair and respectful behavior when playing a sport

Read More

Freeman, Gary. *Motocross.* Radical Sports. Chicago: Heinemann Library, 2003.

Hendrickson, Steve. *Supercross Racing.* Motorcycles. Mankato, Minn.: Capstone Press, 2000.

Schaefer, A. R. *Motocross Cycles.* Wild Rides! Mankato, Minn.: Capstone Press, 2002.

Useful Addresses

American Motorcyclist Association
13515 Yarmouth Drive
Pickerington, OH 43147-8273

Canadian Motorcycle Association
P.O. Box 448
Hamilton, ON L8L 1J4
Canada

MotoWorld Networks Inc.
117 Governor's Square Parkway
Fayetteville, GA 30215

Internet Sites

FactHound offers a safe, fun way to find Internet sites related to this book. All of the sites on FactHound have been researched by our staff.

Here's how:

1. Visit *www.facthound.com*
2. Type in this special code **0736824383** for age-appropriate sites. Or enter a search word related to this book for a more general search.
3. Click on the **Fetch It** button.

FactHound will fetch the best sites for you!

Index